The Magic Cloud

By

Olivia Salmouni

Grosvenor House
Publishing Limited

All rights reserved
Copyright © Olivia Salamouni, 2024

The right of Olivia Salamouni to be identified as the author of this work has been asserted in accordance with Section 78 of the Copyright, Designs and Patents Act 1988

The book cover is copyright to Olivia Salamouni

This book is published by
Grosvenor House Publishing Ltd
Link House
140 The Broadway, Tolworth, Surrey, KT6 7HT.
www.grosvenorhousepublishing.co.uk

This book is sold subject to the conditions that it shall not, by way of trade or otherwise, be lent, resold, hired out or otherwise circulated without the author's or publisher's prior consent in any form of binding or cover other than that in which it is published and without a similar condition including this condition being imposed on the subsequent purchaser.

This book is a work of fiction. Any resemblance to people or events, past or present, is purely coincidental.

A CIP record for this book
is available from the British Library

ISBN 978-1-80381-845-0

Contents

The Enchanted Forest of Dreamland Kingdom	1
The Mystical Cottage	7
The Fairy Who Lived in the Cottage	10
The Witch Who Lived in the Cottage	13
The Magic Cloud	16
The Dragon who Attacked Dreamland	19
The Troll who Attacked Elves	24
The Attack of Hettra	31
Nectar the Fairy	46
Tea with Princess Alice	59
The Royal Wedding	68

The Enchanted Forest of Dreamland Kingdom

Once upon a time in Dreamland, there was a magical kingdom surrounded by a wondrous forest.

The forest was filled with tall, blooming trees. Their branches danced in the blowing wind, making a soothing sound like music to the ears. A vibrant glow of colours emerged from the leaves, shining bright in the atmosphere. It looked like a rainbow on a bright sunny day.

Tiny mushrooms served as homes for the elves, constructed entirely from leaves and branches. From beds to windows, everything was carefully made by the elves, creating their cozy little homes.

The enchanted forest boasted various flowers, some considered unusual, while others were downright magical. Some flowers were upside down, with roots facing upwards, while others refused to

bloom unless given a secret password. There were even flowers with elongated stems, allowing you to climb up and capture a sight of the world around you.

A sight to remember was the white chocolate waterfall, forming a perfect chocolaty stream. During the week, unicorns would visit to enjoy the delicious chocolaty waterfall, while rainbow swans danced on the banks to tranquil music every day. Fairies spent time with animals by the river, using their wands to feed them with white chocolate.

When night fell, the trees glistened as moonlight fell onto them, and stars sparkled above, creating a pure treat for the eyes. As the night grew darker, pink reindeer would come out of their dens, singing lullabies in their soft voices, lulling everyone into a deep sleep.

As the night passed and dawn approached, the sun would rise, and birds chirped and danced in shapes, making it look like a heart floating in the air.

The enchanted forest was a secret, magical place inaccessible to humans, providing a safe haven for its residents. All the magical creatures could, however, see and feel humans every day, sometimes even granting a few of their wishes.

The Mystical Cottage

In the heart of the enchanted forest, where the sunbeams played hide-and-seek with the leaves, a magical cottage stood tall. It was more than just a dream; it was a gleaming cherry-red wonder with patterns that danced in the sunlight. A baby mushroom chimney perched on top, proudly exhaling soft puffs of fairy-friendly smoke. Yellow steps, as cheery as the morning sun, guided curious visitors to the heart-shaped door. The handle, a sparkling delight covered in elegant diamonds, winked as if sharing a magical secret.

Upon crossing the enchanted threshold, eyes were greeted by an extraordinary sight. Floating shelves held a rainbow of wands, bubbling cauldrons, spell books filled with glittery wonders, and fairy teardrops.

Secret jars, tucked behind magic potions, cradled human wishes waiting to unfold.

In the heart of this mystical abode lived Bella, a kind witch, and her dearest friend, Betty, a sprightly little fairy. Their days were a medley of laughter and joy as they played with magical creatures in the enchanted garden. Picture this: the morning sun kissing their chocolate cakes, laughter echoing as they sat on moss-covered benches, smiles adorned with chocolate fudge.

As the sun dipped below the horizon, the cottage transformed into a haven of enchantment. Velvety chairs awaited the duo for movie nights, accompanied by sizzling sausages that danced on their plates. Imagine the giggles and gasps as the friends enjoyed tales woven with magic and mischief.

At dusk, the enchanted forest creatures gathered like old friends around the mystical cottage. Conversations flowed, filled with the day's adventures and dreams of making the forest an even more magical place.

The Fairy Who Lived in the Cottage

Betty, her dress sparkling with each step, tip-tapped with her purple shoes, adorned with a cherry on top. Gold tights shimmered as the sun kissed them, making her pink highlights stand out in her blond hair. With her favorite magic wand and an exquisite crown, she stepped into the enchanted forest to meet all the magical creatures who knew her well.

Unicorns, her beloved companions, would leap with joy at the sight of her. As they danced, Betty's shiny pink wand worked its magic, conjuring up delicious milkshakes, and in return, she showered her unicorns with affection.

Betty cherished her magic wand dearly. A shiny pink treasure that could whip up her favorite meals in no time. It was a commonly known fact that her favorite hobby was baking. From macaroons to muffins and cookies to cakes, the magical wand helped her bake anything her heart desired.

Whenever the enchanted forest faced trouble, Betty would use her wand to protect its creatures. In her kind heart, she used the shiny magic wand to grant wishes to those in need.

One stormy night, as darkness enveloped the forest, a thick fog spread. Betty, brave and determined, wielded her amazing magical wand, saving the enchanted forest from lurking shadows. With a wave of her wand, she guided lost creatures home. Since that night, Betty became a hero known to every corner of the enchanted forest.

The Witch Who Lived in the Cottage

Bella, known for her gentle nature, had peachy skin and dark purple hair with bright pink strands that fell just above her shoulders. She always wore a long, shimmery black hat, and three things were always by her side: a magic wand for emergencies, a cauldron for urgent potion-making, and her magical broom, which could fly her anywhere she commanded.

Unlike most witches, Bella was generous, and her attire consisted of a beautiful black dress with little red roses embossed on it. Sometimes, when going on an expedition, she wore her invisible cloak. Her favorite colour was green, representing the lush greenery of the enchanted forest, and she always painted her nails green. A little bracelet made of gems with her name on it adorned her wrist, which she would fidget with when feeling anxious.

Bella enjoyed riding unicorns, especially her favourite, Olivia. They raced around the forest, played together, and afterward, Bella would feed Olivia chocolate cake. The mystical creatures in the forest loved Bella's flawless and clear voice. Her words rolled perfectly off her cherry-red lips, and her laughter had a sweet energy that enchanted everyone.

A meticulous witch, Bella spent days on her kitchen floor experimenting with spells and potions. The floating shelves in the cottage were filled with spell books and potion bottles waiting to be used. Bella aimed to be the most powerful witch in the kingdom, spending nights studying and experimenting. Some days, the kitchen floor would be a mess, but on others, she successfully made potions to heal injured creatures. Bella knew that spells needed to be perfect, so she worked hard on them. At times, she giggled when she remembered turning a baby unicorn into a little frog and the time it took to fix that error.

The Magic Cloud

On a sunny day, Bella and Betty decided to make magic potions together. With their amazing powers, spell books, and magic wands, they were excited to work on a special potion.

POOF! A horn-shaped bottle burst open, covering the two friends in golden fairy dust. Both girls giggled with joy.

Confidently, the duo continued working and created the most exciting potion in a giant cauldron. POOF! A big pile of dust covered them, the biggest one yet, turning their faces a dazzling violet.

The new potion contained unicorn hair, sticky chocolate syrup, shimmery flower petals, ground rocks from a magical mountain, and fairy teardrops. As they mixed the contents, something magical happened for the first time in the enchanted forest.

THUD! A loud sound filled the entire forest. The ground trembled like there was an earthquake. The sun disappeared behind a vicious storm, casting darkness onto the tall trees. Like a raging bull, a fierce wind blew off the neighborhood elves' mushroom roofs. Bella and Betty ran out of the cottage to see thunder and lightning enclosing the forest. Branches swayed due to heavy winds, and white clouds turned grey. Betty frantically waved her wand in the air, trying to stop the storm.

Bella and Betty's hearts raced with terror. As they regretted making the new potion, a magnificent white cloud descended from the sky. Shimmering like a diamond, the cloud seemed alive and beckoning. Bella and Betty, standing alongside cautious residents, were wonderstruck. It didn't take long for them to realize that with the powerful new potion, they had created a magical cloud that could grant wishes.

The Dragon who Attacked Dreamland

Dreamland was a peaceful kingdom where nobody went hungry. It was ruled by a princess called Alice, known for her kindness and beauty. She invited all the poor residents to a feast every day.

The castle, situated in the center of the enchanted forest, with its beautiful garden of vibrant gold and violet flowers, was gigantic. The royal guards, handsome in their shiny blue uniforms, stood tall at the castle gate to protect it.

The residents of Dreamland were smart and clever, dedicated to their work. The children went to school and studied hard, guided by kind and helpful teachers. Love and harmony filled every corner of Dreamland.

But one fine day, a loud noise jolted everyone awake.

"Roar!" A fierce creature appeared – a deadly dragon with pointy teeth, massive wings, sharp claws, and firm scales. It attacked Dreamland, spitting out blazing fire that burned houses and gardens. The residents cried for help as smoke filled the sky.

Princess Alice sent brave knights to fight the dragon, but they failed. Despite their efforts, the dragon wreaked havoc. The terrified residents hid, praying for someone to save them.

In the midst of destruction, Princess Alice sat in the castle tower, feeling helpless. When she tried to confront the dragon, it roared aggressively, forcing her to step back. Disappointed, she dropped at the doorstep and mumbled a sad song.

"My Kingdom is burning in red flames,

My heart weeps in great pain.

Oh, heaven, bring a miracle!

Make my wish come true,

Banish this dragon, I beg of you!"

POOF! Suddenly, the gigantic, fluffy cloud created by Betty and Bella appeared. It cast a sparkly glow, and Alice felt a rush of adrenaline. The cloud shone at the dragon, blinding it. The dragon roared and fell, defeated by the cloud's mystical power.

The residents of Dreamland celebrated with a grand feast. It became the most lavish celebration, and the fluffy white cloud was hailed as the magic cloud that granted wishes to those in need, reaching far beyond the kingdom's borders. Songs and stories were dedicated to its honor.

The Troll who Attacked Elves

The elves of the enchanted forest lived happily in their cozy mushroom cottages, where they would sing, dance, and laugh together. They wore special mushroom cups and dresses that matched their hats, creating different hairdos every day, sometimes resembling the ribbons on a birthday present. The little elves loved mischief, often pranking each other with their pointy ears. They were talented painters and crafters, creating magical objects for their friends, who loved their customized gifts.

One sunny day, two tiny elves, Rose and Poppy, sat in a flowery meadow singing a cheery song while dangling their feet and waving their hands in harmony.

"Happy as a clam,

Hello world, here I am!

A grin like a Cheshire cat,

It makes my heart burst to chat.

We live in the shadows of the trees,

Dancing around with stripy bees!

Our footsteps are so light,

You would not hear us in the darkest night."

"Do you know what worries all the tiny elves?" asked Rose.

"Not that I can think of. What could it be?" answered Poppy.

"Have you heard about the gigantic trolls that supposedly exist a few miles away?" asked Rose in a worried tone.

"There is no such thing as trolls!" Poppy exclaimed.

"Haven't you heard the old lady elf warning everyone about the trolls? Rumor has it that it is dangerous to go beyond the forest!" Rose explained.

"Oh, c'mon, Rose! Do you believe it? These are just foolish tales. No elf has ever seen a troll with their own eyes!" Poppy rolled her eyes.

"It is true, Poppy. I have heard about animals vanishing and the scary trembling of the ground whenever a troll approaches!" Rose informed Poppy about the past events.

Poppy remained silent.

The enchanted forest had been peaceful until peculiar happenings started occurring. Some creatures were missing, and others heard loud growls at night. All signs pointed to the trolls waking up, striking terror in the enchanted forest.

One night, a loud thumping of footsteps jolted everyone awake. The elves trembled with fear as a hideously broad face appeared out of a dark shadow.

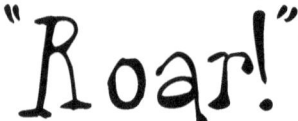

the troll screeched, sending shivers down the spines of the little elves. The troll caused massive destruction, ripping flowers, chewing mushroom cottages, and swallowing them down his blood-red throat. Rose and Poppy, playing tag in the field, spotted the troll.

"The troll is here! I warned you they are real!" Rose exclaimed.

"Oh no! I should have believed you, Rose. I am sorry! What do we do now?" Poppy asked in confusion.

"We don't have time to think, let's just run!" Rose yelled as the troll approached closer.

"Let's go and hide somewhere before we get crushed!" Poppy bellowed as the two little elves ran for their lives.

"Rose, there is a small dark den. The troll would not be able to catch us there. Let's go!" Poppy suggested. Both elves ran towards the den, panting and screaming with fear.

The troll, strong and ferocious, withstood all attempts by the mystical creatures to stop him. The forest was in chaos. Thunder and lightning struck as heavy winds blew, raining cats and dogs. An unusually huge cloud hovered over the forest, covering it with fog. Confused, the troll tried to get rid of the rain and felt scared. As the rain stopped, the cloud shone the brightest light, leaving a shimmering trail of rainbow behind.

"Aaaaarrrrghhhh!"

The troll was terrified and cried out loud. He ran out of the forest as fast as he could. The troll could not tolerate the magical powers of the cloud, created by Betty and Bella. The creatures stared in disbelief. The cloud and fog disappeared, and the forest went back to normal. The mystical creatures cheered as the day had been saved by the magical mighty cloud.

The Attack of Hettra

On a rather chilly autumn morning, the two inseparable friends, Bella and Betty, sat side-by-side on a cheerful pink log, humming tunes. In the heart of the enchanted forest, they joyously cast spells and experimented with magical potions. Nestled near a crackling fire, they toasted marshmallows and sipped on delightful pink lollipop tea during their breaks.

As the sun dipped towards the horizon, the girls gazed at the sky, their eyes shimmering with delight. The heavens transformed into a fiery palette of red and orange, accompanied by the sweet melodies of birds singing lullabies to their fledglings. The blossoming flowers danced in the gentle breeze, creating a magical atmosphere. It was a moment of pure enchantment.

"This sunset is one of the most beautiful I've ever seen!" gasped Bella.

"It truly is a feast for the eyes!" sighed Betty in amazement. "Guess what, Bella? I've gathered some of your favorite mushrooms for dinner tonight!" Betty added with generosity.

"Oh, you did? That's so kind of you, Betty! Where did you find them?" Bella asked, excitement lacing her words.

"I stumbled upon them beneath the oak tree near our cottage. It seemed like the biggest batch of the season!" Betty replied with a soft smile.

"Yummy! I adore mushrooms, especially in soup. How about making mushroom soup tonight? What do you think?" Bella exclaimed with enthusiasm.

"Absolutely! Mushroom soup is perfect to defend against the cold of the night!" Betty replied gleefully.

"Yay! I love trying new things. Another adventure awaits us tonight, and I'm thrilled!" Bella giggled with delight.

"The first of many more to come!" Betty clapped her hands in excitement.

In a hushed tone, Bella shared, "You know, there's someone else who loves mushrooms too."

"Who might that be?" inquired Betty.

"My aunt. She's a witch like me, but unfortunately, an evil one. She doesn't eat mushrooms but uses them in her poisonous potions and spells," Bella disclosed.

"Oh my!" Betty exclaimed with concern.

"She used to be a good witch, but one day, a poisonous frog bit her. Despite everyone's efforts, the poison couldn't be removed. As she grew older, she turned into the evilest witch!" Bella explained with a touch of sadness.

"What's her name?" asked Betty.

"Her name is Hettra," replied Bella.

"She wants to rule the world by turning everyone into her servants!" Bella shared the grim truth.

"Could she come to our enchanted forest?" Betty asked with fear.

"I have no idea. I've never met her, and I hope I never do!" Bella prayed.

Hettra, the wicked witch, was old and frail, with dull, deathly warts covering her skin. She cackled at every minor thing, relishing spider soup while draped in all-black attire. Utilizing black magic, she reveled in causing suffering, disappearing when the moon and stars illuminated the darkest hours of the night.

Hettra's dwelling was haunted, occupied by ghosts and malevolent spirits aiding her in spreading misery. Her abode was draped in cobwebs, infested with spiders. Rumor had it that those who ventured inside never emerged alive.

Three kittens accompanied Hettra, though her attempts to train them in evil practices weren't successful. Their evil meows echoed throughout the day, instilling fear in all creatures. She tested wicked potions on them, feeding them black milk with a pungent aroma of fish.

Capturing and torturing creatures, Hettra imprisoned them in filthy cages, mumbling spells while planning her dark deeds. With her rotten teeth and nails, she displayed hostility, using her dark magic to inflict harm. No traces of kindness existed within her.

Hettra, infamous for invading kingdoms and forests, used her dark magic to poison rulers, casting spells of deep sleep. Villages would awaken to find their homes engulfed in smoke, cobwebs, and filth.

Fearful, they'd succumb to Hettra's will as she sang a hypnotic song:

"Look into my eyes, you cowards,

You are falling asleep.

You will worship me from now onwards,

After you wake up from your deep sleep."

In the dead of night, a bright light shone from Hettra's haunted house, emanating from a green waxy candle casting eerie shadows on damp brick walls. Shelves lined with poisonous green bottles and creeping tarantulas created a scary scene.

Frustrated, Hettra spent hours on the cold floor, attempting to concoct a powerful spell. Her failed attempts only fueled her anger. Determined to regain her power, she ranted, "My spells must work! It's been nine years since I invaded any kingdom. I must do it again!"

Hettra knew that to raise her powers, she needed to extract joy from mystical creatures. Despite reluctance, she eyed Dreamland as her next target, unwilling to

attack the Kingdom of Dreamland due to her niece, Bella. Dreamland became her chosen destination.

As Hettra prepared for the attack, her kittens mischievously played with her magical items. One bit her broomstick, another scratched potion bottles, while the third rolled in the dust, spreading it across her possessions.

The journey to Dreamland was exhausting for Hettra. Travelling on her magical broom through rocky mountains, deserts, and freezing glaciers, she arrived worn-out. Observing Dreamland's radiant castle and the enchanted forest, she momentarily admired the beauty before snapping back to her malevolent agenda.

"I will attack when they least expect it, under the cloak of night!" she laughed wickedly.

Hiding in a small cave, Hettra couldn't resist exploring the kingdom she planned to conquer. As midnight approached, she entered, captivated by the glistening castle and a captivating garden with a white chocolate fountain.

Soaring on her broom across Dreamland, she witnessed unicorns playing in meadows, elves fetching water, and the cottage of her niece, Bella. Peeking inside, she saw Bella and Betty sleeping peacefully by the fireplace. Hettra stared, imagining a life of peace, but the reality of her quest for power snapped her back to cruelty.

Meanwhile, Bella sensed an ominous presence, her fear alerting her. Waking Betty, she whispered urgently, "Something's wrong, Betty. I feel an evil presence – Hettra, my aunt!"

"Your *what*?" Betty screamed in fear.

"Hettra won't stop until she gets what she wants. She's known for stealing happiness from kingdoms to feed her power. And this time, I am sure it's Dreamland!" Bella revealed with urgency.

"Let's save our land now! What are we waiting for?" Betty grabbed her wand, ready for action.

The two friends packed essentials in a frenzy – arrows, water, poisonous berries, and a first-aid kit. Marching out, they nudged sleeping creatures, chanting a wake-up song:

"Wake up, dear creatures,

There is danger.

In the forest, there is a stranger!"

Chanting, they awakened nine elegant white swans, creating a magical mist of shimmery feathers that made elves sneeze, jolting them awake.

Creatures of the enchanted forest mobilized, preparing for Hettra's attack. Bella and Betty, wielding magic wands, scanned the sky to locate Hettra. Bella, torn by her family connection, wished for change.

"I wish Hettra wasn't an evil witch," she muttered.

Bella called upon their magic white cloud for help. With a *POOF!* the cloud materialized in a pool of gold dust, asking, "How can I help you?" Fluffier and adorned with a pinkish blush and bow, the cloud awaited Bella's request.

"I want Hettra to be kind and free of all evil. I want her to be a good witch again!"

Meanwhile, Hettra, roaming in shadows, plotted to capture creatures to fuel her powers. With a sinister laugh, she claimed, "I'm going to be the most powerful witch! I'm coming for you!"

As she laughed, the magic cloud appeared, turning blue and unleashing a torrential downpour across Dreamland. The rain possessed the power to cleanse Hettra's curse, making her blind to her surroundings.

Fuming, Hettra felt changes starting from her face. Warts washed away, replaced by rosy cheeks. Dirty clothes became clean, and her hair turned shiny. The blackness in her heart disappeared, replaced by kindness and compassion and empathy.

Understanding the transformation, Hettra gasped. She was no longer evil, possessing a beautiful heart that craved love and kindness. The mighty white cloud had saved the day once again.

Nectar the Fairy

As time passed, with autumn giving way to winter and then spring, the air resonated with the joyful melody of chirping birds. Unicorns playfully nudged awake the drowsy cows, prompting them to ring their golden bells. The weather exuded a soothing warmth, and the sun painted the sky with its radiant beams. The flowers swayed gracefully in the gentle breeze, their vibrant colors spreading joy and happiness throughout the enchanted land.

This year's spring brought an unusual heat for the elves, leading them to seek refuge in the coldest pond. Some elves lazed about, donning cool sunglasses, while others floated in the still water on bright pink flamingo floaties. Amidst this lively scene, Betty and Bella, dressed in their best attire, sat on a picnic blanket next to a steaming pot of tea. They indulged in scrumptious waffles dipped in chocolate, surrounded by the fragrant aroma of the roses Bella had just plucked from their flower garden.

As they savored the delightful moment, Betty and Bella excitedly planned for the upcoming summer. Betty, adorned with a fancy hat boasting a sky-blue feather, looked at Bella as she admired a vase filled with fragrant roses, setting the stage for the anticipation of a special visitor.

"Do you think Nectar will like all the things we have prepared for her?" Bella asked in a hushed tone.

"I am sure she will. I am really excited because this will be our first visitor in four years!" exclaimed Betty.

Impatience filled the air as the two friends eagerly awaited the arrival of Nectar. To temper their excitement, Bella reminded Betty to calm down, fearing they might inadvertently scare away their special guest. Stretching out on a white and red picnic blanket, the girls poured themselves refreshing lemonade, gazing up at the pretty blue sky and a flock of birds gracefully soaring above.

Suddenly, a bright light appeared, dazzling in its brilliance – like the midday sun when stared at directly. Though small, the light emanated no heat, maintaining a clean, shiny appearance as if it had just emerged from the bubbliest bath in the world. Drawing nearer, it transformed into a tiny fairy, and Betty couldn't contain her joy – it was Nectar! Landing gracefully on the soft green grass, her wings spread wide, Nectar marched toward Betty and Bella's blanket.

"You are so beautiful!" the girls gasped loudly.

Nectar, a ray of sunshine, with teeth like pearls, hummed like a hummingbird, observing the sun twinkle like a star. Her peaceful demeanor radiated through her dazzling diamond eyes, while her golden hair cascaded like threads of real gold.
A robin landed on her pinkie, received a kiss, and gracefully flew away. Nectar wore a gorgeous dress, pinked and rimmed with blue, along with a stunning long cape draped gracefully over her straight shoulders.

In the tiny town of Honeywee, Nectar's home, various fairies lived harmoniously. Residing in a gigantic flower and nourishing herself on honeysuckles, Nectar experienced a world where everything was fresh, clean, and wondrous.
Each fairy in Honeywee was beautiful and kind, contributing to the overall peace and happiness of the community.

However, the most extraordinary element was her magic wand, changing colors in response to her mood and the feelings of others. With a flick of her wand, Nectar could alter the mood of creatures, dispelling feelings of sadness or stress with ease.

Betty and Bella reveled in their time with Nectar, joyfully dancing around a pretty picnic, picking the most beautiful daisies on an enormous hill, and playfully chasing purple and pink butterflies. The highlight for them came when Nectar emotionally shared stories of Honeywee, describing gorgeous blossoming trees, sparkly blue roads, fairies of different types, and the tireless efforts of wise teacher fairies working towards peace and happiness for all.

As happy as puppies with two tails, the three friends chattered and played perfectly until dawn. Sadly, it was time for Nectar to return to Honeywee. Reluctantly, they exchanged hugs and goodbyes.

After Nectar's departure, Betty and Bella resumed their usual lives. Several weeks later, a sparkly mail dropped into their pink and purple mailbox. It was a letter from Nectar.

Dear Betty and Bella,

It was an absolute pleasure to see you both last time. I really enjoyed playing with you two. The food was scrumptious. I've been talking about it all week to my friends repeatedly.

Quite a few things have changed in Honeywee. There are evil slithering snakes swarming around us in their thousands. Their fangs are so sharp that they rip thick branches in half. At the end of their tails, there's invisible poison that could kill an army.

I need everyone's help to defeat these monsters quickly, or we are the ones who will become the prey. We need all your powers to fly like butterflies to our rescue and don't delay!

See you soon.

Love Nectar

xxx

The pair were alarmed, prompting them to frantically pack for the journey. Tiny bottles filled with clever potions, food, and drinks were accompanied by scary weapons. The bags also held various vials, including sleeping and sneezing powders, in hopes they would aid in defeating the impending threat.

The journey was long and tiring, taking Betty and Bella through gloomy woods, scorching deserts, and rich kingdoms. They traveled in a big, brown, dusty carriage, equipped with a wobbly table and sofas that jiggled continuously.

Suddenly, dim lights appeared in the distance. Drawing closer, Betty and Bella discovered a tiny broken village, blanketed in a wintery chill. Houses were crushed, trees chomped, and a big hole in the road revealed horrifying snakes stomping through the remnants. Soot-black trees swayed in the wind as hundreds of cruel snakes angrily hissed above mini houses.

Bella swooped forward to assist the downhearted fairies, with elder fairies wisely battling the vicious snakes. The little ones sought hiding spots, attempting to evade the relentless predators.

"Hiss!" the snakes often said, cleverly inducing fear to halt the fairies' resistance.

Betty and Bella attempted to use a death potion, but Bella noticed they had included the wrong ingredient. Swiftly, they switched to a sneezing potion, applying it

to the cold-blooded monsters. However, an unexpected twist occurred – the snakes started sneezing and spitting poison all around them.

"Hide! Run!" The snakes were quick to bite, their super sharp fangs capable of suffocating a hundred men in one go. They hissed with a curious sound that sent chills down the spine.

All the snakes, coiled or wriggling in the mud, prompted screams and desperate pleas for help from the fairies. Nectar, Betty, and Bella struggled to find a solution, distributing weapons and encouraging the fairies in their battle against the relentless, slimy invaders.

Every attempt proved futile; despite the fairies' efforts, the snakes' hard and slimy skin felt no pain. Even the magical powders failed to produce the desired effect. Despair settled over the defeated village, contrasting with the recently cleaned streets.

Suddenly, a tornado descended from the sky, followed by the puffy cloud that appeared extraordinarily sparkly, fluffy, and even foamy. It was the magic cloud!

The grotesque snakes gasped, growling in reaction. Betty and Bella, undeterred, stuck out their tongues at the snakes. The magical cloud, carefully turning purple, conjured a storm that darkened the sky. Thunder echoed through the miserable atmosphere, and the snakes, bewildered, zigzagged in confusion.

As the sky turned extra dark, the concentrated cloud unleashed a lightning storm, burning the snakes to tinder. The world returned to normalcy, and the next day saw a jubilant celebration in Honeywee.

When the festivities concluded, Betty and Bella safely returned to the Dreamland Kingdom and the enchanted forest they called home. After many weeks passed, a letter dropped into their mailbox – a message from Nectar!

My Dear Betty and Bella,

We have defeated the slithering, scaly, slimy snakes!

The venomous, vicious, violent ones!

Wooooohoooo! Hooray! Be gone, the monsters!

When you came to Honeywee, you warmed our hearts.

You made us brave, strong, powerful!

The snakes were wrapping me with unhappiness.

The village was like an iceberg floating in horror.

Your powerful, perfect, pretty, puffy cloud pulled us out of terrifying danger!

Everyone is saved!

The stories will be written, and music played in the name of the magic cloud!

Excitement bubbled within Betty and Bella as they peeked into the envelope that contained Nectar's letter. To their delight, nestled inside the envelope was a magical token – a precious gift from their fairy friend to express her appreciation.

The token sparkled with enchantment, like a tiny star caught in a dewdrop. Its surface gleamed in shades of pink and blue, as if it held the very essence of a magical sunset. The edges were adorned with delicate swirls, resembling a gentle breeze weaving through the flowers in a meadow.

As the girls held the token in their hands, a soft warmth radiated from it, filling their hearts with a sense of joy and wonder. The center of the token revealed a tiny, intricate image of a hummingbird, wings frozen mid-flutter as if caught in a magical moment.

Nectar had explained in her letter that this magical token held special powers. Whenever Betty and Bella needed a sprinkle of happiness or a dash of courage, all they had to do was gently rub the hummingbird on the token. Its magical energies would then surround them, bringing a touch of enchantment to their day. With wide smiles, the girls admired their newfound treasure, grateful for Nectar's thoughtful gift.

Tea with Princess Alice

One day, Betty and Bella woke up to a sunlit morning in the Dreamland Kingdom, feeling a sense of excitement tingling in the air. Their thoughts were filled with the adventures that awaited them, but little did they know that today would bring a magical surprise.

As they strolled through the enchanted forest, their eyes sparkled with curiosity and wonder. Suddenly, a burst of glittering light enveloped the path before them, and as the glow subsided, they found themselves in a clearing adorned with vibrant flowers and fluttering butterflies.

In the midst of this enchanting scene stood Princess Alice.

She wore a gown woven with threads of moonlight, and her golden crown shimmered like a cascade of sunbeams. With a warm smile, Princess Alice extended her hand and invited the girls to join her in the magical tea party.

"Welcome, dear friends! I've been eagerly waiting for guests to arrive," she exclaimed with a regal grace that matched the beauty of her surroundings.

Betty and Bella were overjoyed, their eyes wide with amazement. Princess Alice gestured towards a table set with the most delightful array of treats. There were cupcakes adorned with edible flowers, cookies that sparkled like stars, and a rainbow of teas that emitted fragrances of strawberries, vanilla, and mint.

"Please, make yourselves comfortable," Princess Alice invited, and the girls eagerly took their seats at the table. As they settled in, magical creatures emerged from the surrounding forest, adding an extra layer of enchantment to the scene. Fairies with white wings fluttered about, and tiny pixies danced on the table, their laughter harmonizing with the rustle of leaves.

Princess Alice poured a tea that shimmered like liquid moonlight into delicate cups adorned with golden stars. The scent of the tea was both comforting and invigorating, promising an adventure for the senses. With a wave of her hand, the princess initiated a joyous melody that echoed through the enchanted clearing.

The tea party began, and laughter filled the air as Betty, Bella, and Princess Alice shared stories of their magical world. The cupcakes sparkled with a burst of stardust as the fairies sprinkled their magical dust over the treats. Each bite was a burst of flavors, transporting the girls to realms of sweetness they had never imagined.

The whimsical pixies, mischievous but delightful, engaged in playful antics, performing acrobatics over the teacups and creating tiny fireworks that lit up the sky in a kaleidoscope of colours. Princess Alice joined the fun, her laughter echoing through the magical glade.

Between bites of enchanted treats, Princess Alice shared tales of other kingdoms. She spoke of wise wizards who painted the sky with hues of twilight and magical animals that spoke in riddles. Betty and Bella listened with wide-eyed wonder, captivated by the fantastical world beyond their own.

As the tea party continued, the enchanted tea began to work its magic. A gentle warmth spread through the girls' hearts, filling them with a sense of joy. The air itself seemed to dance with the melodies of the magical creatures, creating an atmosphere of pure delight.

Betty couldn't resist twirling with a mischievous pixie, while Bella engaged in a dance with a friendly butterfly. Princess Alice joined them, and together they moved in harmony with the magical symphony playing in the background.

The table itself seemed alive with magic. Teacups floated in mid-air, pouring tea with a mind of their own. The cookies playfully stacked themselves into whimsical towers, and the cupcakes arranged themselves into a spellbinding display of colors and shapes.

In the midst of the magical show, Princess Alice unveiled a chest filled with mystical treasures. Each trinket held a unique enchantment, from sparkling crystals that shimmered with the reflections of dreams to tiny mirrors that revealed glimpses of distant lands.

"Choose a gift, dear friends," Princess Alice encouraged, and Betty and Bella eagerly reached into the chest. Betty's fingers touched a smooth, silver locket that held the whispers of ancient spells, while Bella discovered a crystal pendant that glowed with the light of a thousand stars.

While the day unfolded, the magical tea party continued, with the clearing bathed in the glow of the setting sun. The fairies performed a breathtaking display of light, creating intricate patterns that danced across the sky. Princess Alice, Betty, and Bella joined hands, forming a circle of friendship that radiated with the magic of the tea party kingdom.

When the final notes of the enchanting melody played, Princess Alice expressed her gratitude to her newfound friends. "Thank you for gracing my kingdom with your presence. May the magic of our tea party stay with you forever."

With a flick of her wand, Princess Alice created a portal that would transport Betty and Bella back to their beloved home. The girls, now adorned with their magical tokens, bid farewell to the enchanted clearing, promising to carry the joy and magic of the tea party with them.

As they stepped through the portal, the magical world faded away, leaving Betty and Bella standing in the familiar surroundings of their house. Yet, their hearts glowed with the warmth of the magical tea party, and the memory of Princess Alice's kingdom lingered like a sweet dream.

The Royal Wedding

One glorious morning, Princess Alice woke with a bright smile. It was eight o'clock, and the sun's rays flooded her princess bedroom with warmth and joy. She eagerly pulled back the white, sparkly curtain, revealing the beauty of her kingdom. The landscape was surreal; bubble-gum pink flamingos stood gracefully in the glassy still pond, and rabbits hopped on the green lawn. Alice opened the window to the joyful melodies of birdsong.

With the grace of a glowing angel, she glided to her wardrobe and adorned herself in a beautiful blue gown. Her mother, the queen, called from the marble dining hall, "My angel, come downstairs."

Descending the winding staircase, Alice joined her mother for a breakfast of fluffy pancakes topped with whipped cream. "Scrumptious!" she squealed with excitement. The day was turning out to be just perfect.

Moving to the balcony, Alice sat on a grassy green bench to soak in the sunshine. Tropical butterflies in vibrant hues fluttered past her. A gentle breeze ruffled her gown, and in front of her, elegant rivers flowed like doves across the kingdom, with swans gliding gracefully. Like a bird, Alice spread her long arms to feel the fresh air.

Her peaceful moment was interrupted by a loud knock on the door. Wondering who it could be so early, Alice mused, "A woodpecker pecking again, or perhaps the rabbits storing their carrots."

Another knock. Alice tiptoed to the door and opened it just a smidge. To her surprise, there stood a charming prince, tall and handsome. Accompanying him were two delightful cats – one red and smelling of paprika, the other blue like blueberries. The cats played with the prince's shoelaces, purring and curling their paws, creating an adorable sight. Alice couldn't help but smile.

Alice and the prince shared a giggle as the air filled with the scents of blueberries and paprika. "They are not just common cats, you know," the prince said shyly. "They can sing calming music, and even birds join in their songs. They can juggle and paint pictures. They are my best friends."

From behind his back, the prince produced a bunch of roses and handed them to Alice. She looked into his kind blue eyes and felt a connection.

Alice soon learned that the charming prince, known as Arthur, had traveled from a faraway land after hearing tales of her brave nature. As they continued talking, Alice's alluring scent of lotus filled the air, and her radiant smile won Arthur's heart.

Together, they went on eight wonderful dates. On their first date, they had a race with snow-white majestic horses and played with Arthur's enchanted cats. The cats were playful that day, with the red one singing a silly song while the blue one did giant leaps in the air, making Alice giggle.

On the second spectacular date, they descended to the castle kitchens, donned chef hats, and baked scrumptious blueberry cakes, decorating them with a raspberry red heart on top. They read each other their favorite books in the meadow behind the castle, acting out characters from fairytales and pretending to be dragons and knights.

Their third date involved painting glorious portraits of each other. As Christmas approached, they decorated gingerbread houses with sticky blue icing and tiny marshmallows, sharing these treats with magical forest creatures and townfolk.

On the fourth fantastic date, they carried a pink sparkly blanket to a forest meadow, chatting, sipping apple juice, and munching on steaming hot apple pie.

Their fifth date involved picking vibrant flowers, and on the sixth, Arthur built two bikes, and they rode into the gorgeous, colorful sunset.

On the sixth date, they put up a Christmas tree, not a normal one, but a royal tree bigger than a house, adorned with lavish decorations and festive songs.

For their seventh date, they ventured into the enchanted forest to visit Bella and Betty. Together, they made potions, played with spells, and Alice loved seeing her friends get along so well with Arthur.

On the eighth date, they invited all the creatures in the forest to the castle for a Christmas-themed feast. Presents were unwrapped, music played all night long, and there was a lot of dancing and spectacular fireworks.

As the days of celebrations continued, Arthur decided it was time to bring out an emerald ring and ask for Alice's hand in marriage. The only problem was that the gem he had his eye on was hidden in a cave on High Straw, the tallest mountain in the world, guarded by fierce yetis. However, it was the perfect emerald to match Alice's beautiful eyes.

On a frosty evening, as the sun began to set, the brave prince embarked on his journey to the snow-capped mountain. Entering a dark and mystical forest, he heard petrifying wolf howls at the big, glowing moon. Arthur's heart raced with fear, wondering if he would be eaten alive by the beasts. Despite his fears, he was determined to fetch the most perfect emerald for the love of his life.

At the end of a weary and windy day, Arthur reached a hidden cave where a rare, enchanting gemstone gleamed like a million stars in the darkest of nights. It was a breathtaking sight. Arthur, astonished, grabbed the most perfect gemstone and prepared to head back to the castle. Suddenly, the cave began to shake, caught in an earthquake.

As Arthur turned around, two massive yetis stomped closer and closer, and the cave grew dark. The yetis had shaggy beards that looked wise and pointy, like large towers covered in snow. Their deep blue eyes were terrifying, and their dirty, yellow, sharp teeth snapped threateningly.

Arthur thought it was the end for him. The immense yetis approached, growling like lions, and the ground shook beneath them. Rocks around the cave wobbled and fell, blocking the exit. Arthur was stuck alone in the dark, surrounded by the clicking sounds of emeralds that fell to the floor and the fierce roars of yetis behind the blocked cave exit!

A horrifying thought crossed his mind: *What if I am stuck here for life, and I never see Princess Alice again!*

Meanwhile, in the castle, Princess Alice was searching high and low for her lovely prince. She wondered where he had gone and grew increasingly worried. Alice asked all the creatures in the enchanted forest, but nobody had a clue. She called his name many times, but no answer came.

Alice felt hopeless. It was ten in the evening, yet Alice was wide awake. An idea crossed her mind – Bella and Betty might help her with magic and spells. They always came up with the best solutions together.

Walking deep into the enchanted forest, Alice finally reached Bella and Betty's tiny house. The witch and fairy were still awake. Together, they held hands and summoned the magic cloud to come to the rescue. And so it did. In a matter of minutes, above their heads, the majestic cloud glistened in the moonlight. Bella and Betty gratefully waved to their faithful friend.

The cloud left as fast as it arrived on its quest to save Arthur. It searched over oceans, rivers, forests, and fields until finally reaching High Straw, the highest mountain in the magic world. Hovering above the emerald cave, the shimmering cloud created a fierce tornado that spun around with mighty force. The tornado scooped up the yetis, lifting them high into the sky. The rocks that blocked the exit followed them. Arthur was free! The second smaller tornado yanked out Arthur and carried him all the way to the Royal Castle in Dreamland.

Alice squeezed Arthur tightly in her arms. Arthur showed his beloved princess the shiny emerald and bent down on one knee. "Will you marry me?" he asked. And of course, she said yes.

Amidst the wedding preparations, Alice couldn't imagine celebrating without her dear friends, Betty and Bella. With excitement, she invited them to be part of this magical occasion, knowing they would add a touch of enchantment to the festivities. The fairies happily accepted the invitation, eager to share in the joyous union of Princess Alice and Prince Arthur.

Finally, the magical wedding day arrived and the kingdom buzzed with excitement. The castle grounds transformed into a wonderland of enchantment. The entrance was adorned with sparkling fairy lights, and colorful flowers danced in the gentle breeze.

The ceremony took place in the Royal Garden, where roses of every color imaginable bloomed. Betty and Bella, dressed in their finest fairy gowns, fluttered around, casting spells to make the flowers sing harmonious melodies. Each petal produced a soft, tinkling sound as if a tiny music box had been hidden within.

The blue and red cats, now part of the royal family, wore tiny crowns made of twinkling stars. As they pranced around, the stars shimmered and sparkled, leaving trails of stardust that hung in the air like a magical mist.

The wedding altar was crafted from intertwined vines, and it sparkled with crystals that refracted sunlight into a spectrum of colors. Betty and Bella worked their magic, causing the vines to gently sway to an invisible melody. It was as if the very nature around them was celebrating the union.

The strawberry wedding cake stood tall and proud, a masterpiece crafted by the fairies. It was adorned with edible flowers that bloomed and closed in rhythm with the couple's heartbeat. As Princess Alice and Prince Arthur cut into the cake, tiny edible butterflies fluttered out, carrying wishes of happiness for the newlyweds.

The ceremony was filled with magical moments. The magic cloud, summoned by Betty, hovered overhead, showering the guests with tiny, glittering raindrops that disappeared before reaching the ground. The raindrops carried the wishes of joy and love.

As Alice and Arthur exchanged vows, Bella conjured a ring of floating, radiant orbs that circled the couple. Each orb represented a promise made, glowing brighter with each heartfelt pledge. The fairies' magic made the air shimmer with love and joy.

When the couple sealed their vows with a kiss, the sky erupted in a burst of colorful fireworks. The fairies, with a wave of their wands, painted the night sky with bright swirls of pink, blue, and gold. The guests clapped and cheered as the magical display lit up the kingdom.

The dance floor, beneath a canopy of twinkling stars, became a magical stage. Betty and Bella, with a wave of their wands, enchanted the floor to ripple like water, adding an extra layer of enchantment to the dance.

The celebration continued with a feast fit for a magical banquet. The fairies filled the tables with treats that shimmered and glowed. Fruits sparkled with fairy dust, and goblets filled with sparkling nectar seemed to change colors with each sip.

To end the night, the fairies orchestrated a grand finale. A rainbow-coloured carriage, pulled by magical butterflies, awaited the couple. As Alice and Arthur climbed aboard, the butterflies lifted the carriage into the air, leaving a trail of rainbow-coloured stars.

The kingdom watched in awe as the newlyweds disappeared into the night sky, their enchanted carriage twinkling like the brightest star. The fairies sprinkled the remaining stardust over the cheering crowd, ensuring that the magic of the wedding lingered in the hearts of all who witnessed the enchanting celebration.

About the Author

My name is Olivia, I am eight years old and I live in London. I love reading, writing stories and drawing. I believe in all things magic.

My daddy works in Ghana, and I am dedicating the royalties of this book to a charity called Achievers Ghana (one of many projects supported by KGL Foundation).

Ghanaian women and girls are often treated as second-class citizens especially in slums.

They are forced to marry at a young age because of religious, cultural and traditional beliefs. The main purpose of Achievers Ghana is to provide a holistic high-quality education, training and other soft skills so girls too can get jobs and become role models for the generation to come.

Other books by author: 'The Flying Bed'

www.ingramcontent.com/pod-product-compliance
Lightning Source LLC
LaVergne TN
LVHW010315070426
835510LV00024B/3395